Contents

Things you can see in autumn

You can see bonfires.

Seasons

What Can You See in Autumn?

Autumn?

Siân Smith

a Capstone company — publishers for children

Raintree is an imprint of Capstone Global Library Limited, a company incorporated in England and Wales having its registered office at 7 Pilgrim Street, London, EC4V 6LB – Registered company number: 6695582

www.raintreepublishers.co.uk
myorders@raintreepublishers.co.uk

Text © Capstone Global Library Limited 2015
First published in hardback 2015
Published in paperback in 2016
The moral rights of the proprietor have been asserted.

Edited by James Benefield and Kathryn Clay
Designed by Richard Parker
Picture research by Tracy Cummins
Production by Helen McCreath
Originated by Capstone Global Library Ltd
Printed and bound in India

ISBN 978 1 406 28321 1 (hardback)
18 17 16 15 14
10 9 8 7 6 5 4 3 2 1

ISBN 978 1 406 28326 6 (paperback)
19
10 9 8 7 6 5 4 3 2 1

British Library Cataloguing in Publication Data
A full catalogue record for this book is available from the British Library.

Acknowledgements
We would like to thank the following for permission to reproduce photographs: Dreamstime.com: © Oseland, 4, © Rsaulyte, 9, 22, © Tab1962, 16; iStock: © kirin_photo, 6, © monkeybusinessimages, 8; Shutterstock: ayosphoto, 20 left, Brent Hofacker, 15, Daniel Schweinert, 13, Dennis Donohue, 19, Firma V, 7, Franck Boston, 20 middle, J. Long, 11, Jacek Chabraszewski, 5, Kuznetsov Alexey, 20 right, L.L.Masseth, 12, Maridav , 14, Richard Schramm, 21, Smit, 17, 22, TessarTheTegu, 18, XiXinXing, 10, back cover.

Cover photograph reproduced with permission of Shutterstock, © S.Borisov.

Every effort has been made to contact copyright holders of material reproduced in this book. Any omissions will be rectified in subsequent printings if notice is given to the publisher.

You can see leaves.

You can see costumes.

rake

You can see rakes.

You can see a scarf.

frost

You can see **frost**.

You can see jumpers.

You can see scarecrows.

You can see pumpkins.

You can see lanterns.

You can see apples.

You can see apple pies.

blackberry

You can see blackberries.

acorn

You can see **acorns**.

You can see squirrels.

You can see birds.

Autumn quiz

Which clothes would you wear in autumn?

The four seasons follow a pattern. Which season comes after autumn?

spring

summer

?

autumn

Picture glossary

acorn

frost

Index

Answer to quiz on page 20: jumpers and scarves
Answer to question on page 21: winter

Notes for teachers and parents

Before reading

Building background: Talk about the seasons of the year. Which season are we in at the moment? Ask children what they would see if they looked out of a window in autumn.

After reading

Recall and reflection: Which season is before autumn? Which season follows autumn? What happens to the leaves on the trees in autumn? Why might a squirrel collect nuts in autumn?

Sentence knowledge: Help the children count the number of words in each sentence.

Word knowledge (phonics): Encourage children to point at the word *can* on any page. Sound out the phonemes in the word *c/a/n*. Ask the child to sound out each letter as they point to it, and then blend the sounds together to make the word *can*.

Word recognition: Ask children to find the word *you* on page 5. How many more times can they find it in the book?

Extending ideas

Sorting leaves: Show children a collection of leaves. Ask them to sort the leaves (e.g. by shape, size, colour, etc.). Ask children to choose a leaf and draw around its outline. Then they should colour in their leaves, trying to match the colours closely.

In this book

Topic words
acorns
apple pies
apples
birds
blackberries
bonfires
costumes
frost
jumpers
lanterns
leaves
pumpkins
rakes
scarecrows
scarves
squirrels

Topic
autumn

High-frequency words
a
can
see
you

Sentence stem
You can see _____.

Ask children to read these words:
scarf   p. 8
frost   p. 9
pumpkins   p. 12